THE
RELIGION
OF JESUS

Escaping the religion of the religious others

RONALD C. GELAUDE

Religion (Greek, *threskeia*): an outward expression of an inward spiritual devotion

Religion (Latin, *regalia*): to bind belief and practice

I'm not sure exactly when or how it happened, maybe it's because of the various events and experiences you will read about in this book, but long before becoming a follower of Jesus, I somehow knew that you could tell what a person truly believed by his or her actions over the course of time—there is an unavoidable binding together of belief and practice.

Therefore, whether we care to admit it or not, each of us is religious.

—Ron

TABLE OF CONTENTS

A Note to the Reader

To whom it may concern…

To those who have given up religion; to those who have lost what it means to be religious; to those who, because of the actions of a few, have no interest in religion; to those who have been wounded, shamed, marginalized, and rejected by it; to those who carry with them the baggage it has created; to those who have suffered much because of it; to those who have thrown religion out the window, who think they are not, and as such, want no part of it—it is for you that this book was written.

As you will see, my study of the extraordinary life of Jesus, a "hat moment" in the Kenyan bush, my cousin Dennis, and the many heart-warming and heart-wrenching events I have experienced in my seventeen years of being a pastor and church planter are the impetuses behind this book.

My hope is that it will in some way speak to you as you read it, as it has spoken to me during its writing.

— *Ron…*

Preface

There are dozens of books out there that proudly claim, without reservation, that Jesus was irreligious or even sacrilegious. I suppose it's in vogue to make such observations, but in reality, nothing could be further from the truth. Jesus's actions and teachings demonstrate that he was a far cry from being irreligious or sacrilegious.

Yes, he was profoundly frustrated and angry with the religious leaders of the day and what religion had become, but his mission was not one of dismissing religion. Jesus regularly observed all of the Jewish religious traditions and ceremonies and celebrated the holidays with great energy and willingness (the Passover meal, worship at the temple, and the reading of the Mosaic Law, just to name a few).

Contrarian that he was, Jesus made his mission one of boldly reclaiming a religion that had morphed into legalism and dogmatism. He came offering a religion of unparallel freedom and unwavering compassion, and it is here that a tangible hope surfaces. There is a religion worth considering, a religion worth *living*.

It's called the religion of Jesus.

Real religion, the kind that passes muster before God the Father, is this: Reach out to the homeless and loveless in their plight, and guard against corruption from the godless world.
— James, the brother of Jesus (James 1:27)

INTRODUCTION

JUST TO BE CLEAR | *the church and its founder*

It is rather clear to me from my observations of what he has created that God is not the author of confusion or disarray—actually, quite the opposite. For example, when you pause and gaze at the vastness of the cosmos and the intricacy of its workings, you can see God's desire for order and design. When it works well, it's a sight to behold.

Life and the cosmos around it are no accident. The same can be said of the church that Jesus founded. Whether we like it or not, the church, which simply means a gathering of students and followers of Jesus Christ assembled for a common purpose, remains the primary avenue by which God communicates his divine message of everlasting hope, wholeness, healing, justice, and truth. At its very core, it too is a series of interdependent systems, or assemblies (congregations), all working in a divinely ordained order. The term *church* speaks to that which is global (the millions of congregations around the globe) and to that which is local (a congregation of six in the remote Kenyan bush).

From the largest of the large to the smallest of the small, every church is still the church. The New Testament writers refer to it as the bride of Christ, his prized possession, his body, his household, his love of loves, and a city on a hill. When it works well, it's a sight to behold.

So, just to be clear, what you are about to read is not a treatise on the church. As one theologian commented, the church, in spite of all its imperfections, bumps, maladies, and challenges, remains the church of Jesus Christ. Be ever so careful how you speak of her.

I repeat: this book is not about the church. As you will see, it's about the religion(s) that people bring to it, and herein rests the grand struggle; it is a battle worth every ounce of energy we can muster, for in a world that is hurting more than ever, the local church is and always will be the source of hope.

Without reservation or hesitation, I believe that the endeavor to understand the religion of Jesus is well worth the effort, but what else would you expect from a pastor?

There are two sides to every question [or story].

— Protagoras (485-410 B.C.)

PART ONE | *The Religions of the Religious Others*

Again the Jews [the religious leaders] picked up stones to stone him, but Jesus said to them, "I have shown you many good works from the Father. For which of these do you stone me?"

—John, one of the apostles of Jesus (John 10:31–32)

INTRODUCTION | religion gone wild, again…

Religion, the intentional or unintentional binding together of what we believe and how we behave, has been part of life since it began. The emergence of animism, the bringing together of the spiritual realm and the physical realm, for example, can be traced back thousands of years. Over the course of human history, six major world religions have emerged: Judaism, Islam, Hinduism, Buddhism, Animism, and Christianity. Each of these religions has a deep, rich, and extremely long history. Along the way, we've been taught that the primary common denominator among all religions is a defined set of beliefs and subsequent behaviors that are, for the most part, good. In other words, the widely held common thread that runs through all religions is good behavior or deeds for the benefit of humanity; these behaviors and deeds are driven by what we actually believe. Supposedly, being *religious* is a good thing.

Having the advantage of experience and knowledge of history, however, we can easily see that there is a more striking common denominator, one that, over time, has tarnished the word *religion*. The challenges and devastation that religion has brought to the world stage are profoundly evident—prejudice, bigotry, judgmentalism, burnings, executions, genocide, hatred, terrorism,

7

wars, imprisonments, slavery, and strife. All have been committed in the name of religion. No religion is exempt; no religion has a corner on the market. A brief review of any religious history book will bear this out. It seems as if every few hundred years or so, religion goes wild, again.

It's a heartbreaking commentary, don't you think?

As an ordained pastor of a Christian denomination, I can only speak to Christianity. Those who lead and serve in the other world religions can and must speak for themselves. This book is limited to the religious dynamics of Christianity. Sadly, it doesn't take much digging to uncover the religious tragedies of the Crusades, the persecution of Jews, the burning of witches, the hanging of African Americans, forced conversions, the bombings of abortion clinics, and the picketing of funerals with "God hates (fill in the blank)" signs—all under the umbrella of Christianity.[1]

My personal favorite and less violent example is the seventeenth-century excommunication of Copernicus and Galileo by the church for suggesting that our solar system was heliocentric as opposed to geocentric. It was the conviction of the contemporary church leadership that these two scientists were heretics because the Bible clearly and quite literally stated that the sun rose in the morning and set in the evening. Therefore, it had to be the sun that rotated around the earth. It took until 1965 for the church to admit its mistake. Unfortunately, there is a similar Bible-versus-science argument taking place today. Once again,

---

1   See appendix I.

because of a strict reading of the Bible, in some Christian circles, if you suggest that the earth is millions of years old, you are accused of heresy. According to how they read the Bible, the age of the earth and the cosmos in which it rests is somewhere in the range of ten thousand to twenty thousand years old.

It's the young-earth theologians versus the old-earth theologians. Regardless of sound scientific inquiry, just as it was in the time of Galileo and Copernicus, the conversation is closed; there is no room for debate. If you dare disagree, you are met with the same ad hominem attacks. The continued science and Bible debate manages to build more religious walls than bridges; this is most unfortunate and, as you will see, profoundly unnecessary.

Furthermore, underneath the same Christian umbrella, you also discover a gross separation of the secular and sacred, and the lingering affects of a Euro-centric approach to global mission work (i.e. to be a true Christian one must deny all of one's cultural beliefs and practices that don't align with the doctrines of a higher church authority on the other side of the globe). All you need to do is pay attention, and you'll see that not much has changed over the years. Is it any wonder that well-intended people are frustrated with religion? It has been my personal experience that being nonreligious or even irreligious is in vogue for those who have ditched Christianity and even for some who still embrace it. This characterized my beliefs at one point. However, have we inadvertently thrown *religion* under the bus? Because of the actions of more than a few, have we mistakenly set aside and ignored the words of James, the half brother of Jesus? "Real religion, the kind that passes muster before God the Father, is this: Reach out to the homeless and loveless in their plight, and guard against corruption from the godless world."[2]

The rest of this book is a less-than-scholarly attempt to recast Christianity in a fresh vision of its original intent, to reclaim that which has been stolen over time by personal agendas, politics, egos, fear, and human nature. My sole desire is to encourage and offer hope to those who have dismissed or given up on the Christian religion and if at all possible, invite them in or back into the mix.

The Christian religion, when running wild in the right direction, is an epic journey of a lifetime. It is one that fills the God-void in our hearts and fuels the furnace of our souls, but as you will see, it's not really about the religions of *Christianity*.

It's about the religion of Jesus, its founder.

---

2   James 1:27 (The Message).

THE RELIGION(S) OF CHRISTIANITY | *the elephant in the room*

We would end up meeting twice a month at a local café for well over a year, and I would watch her fall in love with the Jesus she had never met before, but our very first encounter went something like this:

"Are you a Christian?" she asked with what seemed like a slightly strategic grin on her face.

My mind raced. *How do I answer? It seems like a loaded question. I am...maybe. It's not something I like to admit to anymore. Is it a political question, a theological question, a religious inquiry? What is she really asking? What the heck does that word mean anyway?*

Then she asked me the question of all questions, the iceberg to the Titanic question: "Are you one of those Evangelical Christians?"

I must have passed out in fear, because after this, I don't remember much more of the conversation. By the way, she grew up in a large Christian church where over time she had come to believe that all Evangelicals were more concerned about being doctrinally correct than deeply concerned about the poor, homeless, orphaned, hungry and those dying of HIV/AIDS. It's a common story, isn't it?

It comes as no surprise that what it means to be a Christian today is something far different than what it was a couple thousand years ago; the baggage the "C" word brings with it is at times overwhelming, but not many *Christians* really want to talk about it. There seems to be an elephant in the room.

Over the centuries, the religion of Christianity has taken on many forms, most of which were by no means new. Some of them will be addressed as we explore the religion of Jesus, but for now, let's examine three of the religious challenges that Jesus, the founder of Christianity, faced back in the day. Why? you might ask. It seems as if they are making a resurgence of sorts.

These are the religions of Christianity (a.k.a. the religion of the religious others).

The Religion of the Religious Elite

The religious elite live in a world of religious legalism and control. Their focus is on selling what Dallas Willard[3] calls fire insurance (i.e., demanding people say the right words and repeat the right prayers so they will escape the wrath of God and burning in hell); they speak and preach boldly that certain behaviors mean you're in and speak vehemently against certain behaviors, which mean you're out. The religious elites are alive and well today.

Using my interpretation of this manifestation of religion, I have provided a modern-day rendition of the account of an

---

3   Dallas Willard is a scholar, professor, and author. He wrote Divine Conspiracy, in which he coined the phrases sin management and fire insurance. You gotta love it...

important event in the life of Jesus, as recorded by Luke, a physician who wrote two books of the New Testament:

On one occasion, when Jesus had an audience with a group of religious elites, he shared with them the following story—a story that would reveal the vast difference between them and those whom they considered unworthy of God's love, people who engaged in certain behaviors that meant they were out, people they had written off.

One day, two men went to the biggest church in town to pray. One was a highly respected and well-known senior pastor, and the other was an IRS agent. The IRS agent was considered by most to be traitorous and corrupt; he was hated and held in great disregard. The senior pastor stood up front near the pulpit so he could be seen and heard by the people in attendance and boldly proclaimed with great self-confidence, *"God, I thank you so much that I am not like other people; people like this despicable IRS agent. You know, people who do evil things, people who cheat on their spouse, thieves and traitors. Unlike all of them, even though fasting is only required occasionally, I fast twice a week. Furthermore, I give a full 10 percent of my gross income, and to make sure people see how religious I am, I give it in full sight of all so they can follow my example."*

Unlike the senior pastor, the lowly IRS agent stood in the back, away from the glitz and glamour of it all. He fell on his knees and stared at the floor; covering his face in shame, he cried out, *"Dear God, please find it in your heart to embrace me with your mercy and grace! Please forgive me, for I am one who has fallen horribly short of the love and life you want me to live."*

After the story, looking the religious elite square in the face, Jesus said to them, *"Guess what. It's the IRS agent who made things right with God the Father, not you! Those who promote themselves and boast of their religious behaviors will in the end be humbled by God, but those who simply humble themselves before a loving and graceful God will be lifted up. Yes, the ones you have written off."*[4]

This typifies the religion of the religious elite, and it's alive and thriving today.

My brothers and I grew up in XYZ Bible Church. It was a nice place, and the people were good. Each Sunday, our mom would drag all six of us through the doors. Once there, we would sing some hymns, listen to a sermon, hang out for a while, and then go home. Sometimes, we would go back Sunday night and repeat the cycle, and occasionally, we would go on Wednesday to do the same. As young children, it didn't really bother us. We didn't know any better, but then my younger brother and I entered high school. Church became another place to meet girls—lots of them! I'm certain it's still a common motive for going to church.

Unfortunately, just when we thought the church gig would pay off, the unthinkable happened. Our world was rocked. Our dad became a Christian. After sixteen years of my mom taking us to church solo, our dad was now part of the mix. For a while, it was okay, but then, out of the blue, the wheels fell off the wagon; our parents decided to become members. I remember it as if it were yesterday. My mom, dad, younger brother, and I sat

---

4   Luke 18:9–14.

in the basement of the church with the elders surrounding us; each one had a phonebook-size Bible in hand; it was very weird. As we sat there, they began to ask us lots of questions: Do you drink alcohol? Do you dance? Do you smoke? Do you listen to rock and roll? Do you play cards? Do you read your Bible? Do you gamble? Do you watch bad movies? My brother and I sat there in shock; we didn't quite know how to respond. You see, my brother and I played in a rock-and-roll band (we were really bad), went to Friday night football bashes, danced, drank beer as often as we could, smoked, and played cards with our friends. I remember thinking, *Today we're going to hell!* So, we gathered our thoughts and did what any normal girl-chasing high school kids would do when faced with such a cosmic crisis: we lied. We must have kept straight faces, because after a few nervous moments, we were in; we were members. I can't speak for my brother, but this was when I learned to play the game, say the right words, pray the right prayers, act a certain way on Sundays, and enjoy the praises of the church folks.

To the religious elite, I was a fine, upstanding young Christian man, but in reality, none of it was true.

Over the course of eighteen years of churchgoing, we never talked about helping the poor, the hungry, the homeless, or the orphaned. We never talked about personal brokenness, the baggage of shame, or how to learn and grow from failure. We never talked about social justice, the story of God's reckless love, or how science can reveal the very nature of the living God. It was taboo to suggest that the cosmos might be billions of years in the making. Each week, the service was about the anger of God, saying the prayer, getting into heaven, and not going to hell. It was about not doing this or that, figuring out who was in and who was out; it was about what Dallas Willard calls *sin management.*[5]

This lasted as long as I attended XYZ Bible Church. (There was more than one actual church; we moved every few years.) At the age of eighteen, with great joy, I moved on, tired of being nothing more than a worthless sinner, frustrated at the idea of science and the Bible in conflict and contradiction, sick of being told what to think, exhausted and bored with playing the game.

Jump ahead forty years, I'm a pastor (yes, it's a long story). I'm driving out of my subdivision only to read the sign on the church across the street, which reads, *"Reserve your seat today, smoking or nonsmoking. Repent. Hell is real. Join us on Sunday."* Not much has changed. To the religious elite, it's still only about escaping the fire of hell. The ugly theological lines of division remain, as does the disdain for anyone who may hold to something other than an extremely narrow reading of the Bible or whose belief in how God works differs from theirs and the rejection of the idea that anyone who thinks differently could even be a Christian. These gulfs are as wide now as they were forty years ago.

The religious elite embrace the notion that they've earned their place with God by obeying the rules, saying the right words, believing the right things, and acting a certain way, and

---

5   See footnote 3.

furthermore, anyone who hasn't or doesn't is unworthy and undeserving of God's love and grace. Like the religious leaders of Jesus's day, who believed that God rejoiced at the death of a sinner, the religious elites of today insist that everyone follow the letter of the law (a.k.a. the Bible), but only as they see it; if you're not willing to do so, you're out.

A recent heartbreaking example of this is the religious elite's reaction to Rob Bell's most recent book *Love Wins*.[6] Two dear friends of mine, who are in their twenties and have an unwavering love for and commitment to Jesus, were verbally ridiculed out of a Bible study simply because they read the book and were interested in discussing some of its nuances. Apparently, to the elites, honest inquiry and genuine theological investigation is a sign of spiritual weakness. So, my two friends were out.

Indeed, the religion of the religious elite is alive and well today, but as you will see, this is not the religion of Jesus.

The Religion of the Religious Fanatics

Fanatics take religious elitism and kick it up a notch or two; they embrace a form of religious greed, characterized by conflict, slander, name-calling, shouts of "God hates (fill in the blank)," and a few other ugly behaviors. They love to pick a fight for their so-called Christian cause and are willing to go to any extreme

---

6   Love Wins, by Rob Bell is a book that examines many Christian beliefs and sometimes pushes those beliefs to the limit; it is a book that makes its readers think by gently questioning traditional, long-standing Christian doctrine, especially the issue of hell.

to make their point. A fanatic in this context is one who takes the idea of being zealous for a cause to its extreme. Fanatics are dangerous and do far more damage than they realize. Being zealous for a cause is admirable and necessary to create energy and passion, but zealotry gone wild results in extreme fanaticism.

Just as it is with the religious elites, the religion of the religious fanatics is alive and well today. All you need to do is pay a bit of attention and you'll read or hear about funerals being picketed by fanatics who couldn't care less about those who grieve the loss of a cherished loved one, well-intended church gatherings with picketers carrying "God hates…" signs, clinics being bombed, and gays being persecuted.

Again, the following is my interpretive rendition of a biblical account that demonstrates this version of religion. Mark, another writer of the New Testament, recalled a time when Jesus encountered the religious fanatics of his day.

On one other occasion, Jesus went into the place of worship and noticed a man who was disabled; his hand was disfigured and useless. It was the Sabbath. By the way, this wasn't his first encounter with the religious fanatics. To them, Jesus was a threat and they continually looked for reasons to kill him. Nevertheless, Jesus walked directly up to the disabled man and said, "Stand up in the front of the church so everyone can see." Upon the handicapped man doing so, Jesus asked the religious fanatics, "Which is lawful to do on a Sabbath; to do what you see as good things or what you consider evil things; to save a life any day of the week or to kill, like the plans you have for me?"

Having never been challenged this way before, they stood there in silence. But, on the inside, they were furious. Jesus surveyed them with indignation, distressed that they couldn't care less about a man who had struggled all of his life. He asked the man to stretch out his shriveled hand. Upon doing so, the disabled man's hand was completely restored; imagine the joy and relief that must have raced through this man's heart and soul when he realized that someone actually cared about him.

The religious fanatics, steeped in their hardness and hatred for anyone who threatened their narrow view of God, missed the point of it all and ramped up their plans to kill Jesus by partnering with another group of religious fanatics.[7]

I'm also reminded of the time when the religious fanatics of Jesus's time dragged a woman whom they had caught in the act of having sex with a man not her husband. Pulling her by the hair, naked and shamed, they placed her in front of Jesus and demanded she be stoned to death. "It's written in the Law!" they proclaimed. Jesus, however, put them in their place by inviting all those who were without fault to throw the first stone and then compassionately reached out to this young woman. Taking her by the hand, he showered her with grace and mercy and then strongly suggested that she didn't need to live this way. Imagine the relief and joy that raced through her heart and soul. The

---

7   Mark 3:1–6.

religious fanatics want to throw rocks; Jesus wants to love people where they are.[8] There is indeed a stark and unfortunate contrast between Jesus and the religious fanatics.

It's easy to get caught up in all the religious fervor, hype, and argument. It can be in vogue to throw rocks instead of unconditionally loving others wherever they may be in life. I know this to be true, for there was a time when a rock was my weapon of choice.

His name was Dennis; he was my cousin. Growing up, my younger brother Mike, Dennis, and I were great friends. We had loads of fun together and always found a way to get into the type of trouble typical of kids our age. Later in life, my wife and I would spend time with Dennis when we traveled to San Francisco. We enjoyed our time together, as we would hang out and share stories of the past and then dream about the future. Dennis was gay, and it didn't matter to us. He was my cousin, my good friend. I loved him.

Then I became a Christian, and somehow, it skewed how I viewed my cousin. Our conversations changed; our phone calls grew less and less frequent; our visits were suddenly filled with tension. I had morphed into one of those fanatics, and my rocks were verbal. As it is with the religious elites and fanatics, it became more important for me to be right than loving and compassionate. According to the Bible, being gay was no longer something I should tolerate; in fact, it was now my duty to speak out against

---

8   John 8:2–11.

it. A year or so into it, Dennis informed me that he had come down with HIV/AIDS. It was the eighties, and his prognosis was grim, but my position regarding his lifestyle changed little. Dennis lived on for almost two years, and when he was on his deathbed, I called to ask if I could fly out and visit him. But my dear cousin, the one with whom I once shared many good times, politely said no. That was it; the damage had been done. I never saw him or spoke to him again. He died the following week.

To this day, even at this writing, when I think of Dennis, my heart wells up with grief and regret. It was a gut-wrenching wake-up call that pushed me off the cliff of religious bigotry and judgmentalism; it changed my life and helped me not only see but experience the compassionate hand of a Jesus, who longs to shower all people with love, grace, mercy, and a healing touch. It was a defining moment, and in retrospect, I know that Dennis changed my life. This doesn't sit well with the religious fanatics.

The religion of the religious fanatics is not the religion of Jesus; it would have been so good to realize this much sooner in my walk with him.

The Religion of the Religiously Indifferent

The indifferent simply don't care; their focus is elsewhere, and as far as religion is concerned, they have given up. They're good people. They are spiritual. Some are compassionate, but most are focused on themselves or what's in their best interest. Some are self-absorbed and apathetic toward the rest of the world.

The physician Luke recalls a story told by Jesus that reflects the life of the religiously indifferent. Here's my interpretive rendition.

There was a father who was a well-respected leader in his community; he was a patriarch of sorts with significant wealth. Much to his great pleasure, he had two sons, and he had great hopes for them and their future. One day, out of the blue, the younger son went to his father and demanded his inheritance now! He had grown disinterested in the desires of his father and yet, at the same time, he wanted all that his father had provided him. He had become self-absorbed, all at the expense of his family.

This demand was totally out of line and in any "normal" circumstance the father would have chastised him for being insolent and disrespectful. It was a demand that would cost his father everything: his wealth, his reputation, and his dignity. In this simple request, the father's dreams were shattered, but the younger son didn't care; he had grown indifferent, and life was now all about him.

Surprisingly, this father was different, vastly different from any father in the entire region. At great personal expense, he willingly gave away himself and his fortune. So the younger son, who got exactly what he wanted, left home. Having taken all that really didn't belong to him, he departed for a distant land. In a short time, however, he had managed to squander his father's wealth; he spent it all on wild living without cause or concern for anyone else. It got so bad that he had to hire himself out as a slave; he was hungry and homeless with no place to go. He lost everything.

In the midst of his stupor, he came to his senses and remembered what life was like with his father. So, he humbled himself and returned home. He anticipated a not-so-warm welcome and was willing to start all over again, but when his father saw him coming down the road, he ran out to greet him with great joy. It was not the reception the younger son expected.[9]

In this story, which is really only half of the story, the younger son typifies the religiously indifferent in that the essence and meaning of life is all about them and their own interests, nothing more and nothing less. For a variety of reasons, both good and bad, they have forgotten who it was that created them and have traded their *father's* dreams and desires for the dreams and desires of their own. They have seemingly lost interest in the father; it's a common story, isn't it?

I hear the word *but* quite regularly.

Not that long ago, we had a workday in my neighborhood. We all got together and built a rather impressive landscape wall; it was impressive because none of us really knew what we were doing. It was great fun, and we truly enjoyed the project, so we celebrated our accomplishment with a party—you know, burgers and potato salad; it was a blast. My neighbors are wonderful people; they're good friends and know what I do for a living, so if we hang out long enough, the conversation can get spiritual

---

9   Luke 15:11–24.

(it comes with being a pastor). As we chat, the *but* word begins to emerge: "I grew up in a Christian home and went to church regularly, *but* it left a bad taste in my mouth; *but* I was burned by the pastor; *but* it was meaningless; *but* I saw how Christians hate people; *but* once they exit the doors of the church, the people are hypocrites, mean and intolerant; *but* while they sing a good song on Sunday, they really don't care about the poor, the homeless, and the hungry." I hear the *but* word quite regularly.

These comments typify the religion of the religiously indifferent.

Christianity, as portrayed by the religion of the religious others (the elites and fanatics), is profoundly unappealing to most, and in many cases, it's outright offensive. Because of what has been done under the umbrella of Christianity and those who espouse the religion of the religious others, the religiously indifferent are left to create a religion they can manage or tolerate, one that in essence is the unintentional recreation of God. It's a religion created in their own image (view) of God and life; they think highly of Jesus but for all the aforementioned reasons want nothing to do with religion or Christianity.

Ironically, much like the religiously indifferent, Jesus felt the same way about the religious elites and religious fanatics; he called them a bunch of snakes, whitewashed tombs (looking good on the outside, but empty on the inside), and teachers who burdened people with the weight of heavy stones (endless religious rules and regulations designed to control, stifle, and smother). Jesus was profoundly frustrated with the religious elites and fanatics and what they had done to push people into a life of religious indifference. He recognized that those who had been rejected, written off, disenfranchised, ridiculed, and dismissed, just like the previously mentioned younger son, had given up on the Father and the religion he offers.

Jesus saw their pain, their frustration, and their angst; he sensed their loss of hope and the emptiness they felt as they simply went through the motions of a self-absorbed life. The Gospels of the New Testament record how on many occasions, when Jesus saw the crowds of the now religiously indifferent, he had deep compassion for them. His heart was broken, and they became his personal mission; he would do anything to bring them home, even if it cost him everything—again, much like the father of the younger son.

But it's important to note, even the religion of the religiously indifferent is not the religion of Jesus. Religious indifference is a dangerous philosophy of life; it can breed an apathetic and uncaring spirit. Worse yet, it can lead to a tendency to believe almost anything that sounds good as long as it doesn't demand too much of your time and money. The challenge for the religiously indifferent is four-fold:

1. Core beliefs that guide healthy decision making are moving targets;

2. Self-absorption deadens the emotions, and empathy is the first to go;

3.   Egocentrism quickly gets old to those around you; and

4.   When the bottom falls from underneath you, you're left with nothing and nowhere to go.

This is precisely why, as was stated earlier, when Jesus saw the crowds of the religiously indifferent, he had deep compassion for them. His heart hurt for them, and so they became his personal mission.

As you will see, the religion of Jesus can change everything.

THE RELIGION OF WORDS | *gentlemen, this is a football*

Not too long ago, a few us got together for a visit with my mom (at the time, she was eighty-four). While we were hanging out, making jokes and talking sports, someone used the words *hockey puck*; they seemed innocent enough, but my mom began to laugh. When she explained that the words *hockey puck* had been used by my grandfather to describe excrement, we couldn't contain ourselves. The laughter went on for quite some time. As you can imagine, we began to use my grandfather's terminology in many creative ways; we got a bit carried away.

After the laughter settled, we went into her library and found an old *Merriam Webster's Dictionary* (1948) and began to look up other words to see how they might have changed. We searched it to see if it contained or defined a few popular/new words we use today. This went on for hours. It was rich.

One of the great challenges of present-day Christianity is found in theological words, determining what they *really* mean. Over time, many of them morph into something not intended by those who used them long ago. The meanings change; new ones arrive on the scene, and old ones get lost in the mix of culture and experience. The challenge is understanding the historical setting as well as the linguistic and technical nature of many Christian terms, which were used back in the first century. Many of these terms are abused by today's religious elites and fanatics.

So, before we can get to the religion of Jesus, we must first briefly revisit and recapture three key words that have been lost, stolen, and hijacked over time by culture, agenda, politics, and ego. Before we move forward, however, I want to tell you a story you will not believe, and I need to apologize in advance for the setting in which this story unfolded.

I was on my way home from a conference, a large gathering of church planters who had come together to discuss the issues of leadership, spiritual growth, and effectively reaching out to new people, especially those who have given up on church. It was a two-day conference and well worth the drive. Wanting to get back home quickly, I headed back as soon as the last session ended; it was a long drive. About six hours into it, I needed to stop at the next rest area in order to deal with the many cups of coffee that I had imbibed to keep me awake (you get the picture). As I arrived, there was no time to waste, so I quickly ran into the restroom and stood at the appropriate place to get rid of the coffee (sorry). Standing there, I noticed something on the urinal, right next to the flush handle; you couldn't help but notice it.

Right there in front of me, and on every other urinal in the restroom, was a small flyer outlining how we were all sinners in need of repentance and salvation so we could escape the flames of a burning hell. Unbelievable! Urinal evangelism! Who would have thought? In a twisted way, you have to admire this person's zeal and commitment to efficiency. You can't make this stuff up!

However, this leads us to three key theological and mission-critical words that need to be rescued before we can get to the heart of it all:

- *Salvation* (the God-ordained art of being rescued both *from* and *into*)

When you hear the word *salvation*, what comes to your mind? What images flash before your eyes? From what you see and hear from Christians today, how would you define it? For the longest time, upon hearing that word, I was instantly brought back to a time when it meant nothing more than escaping the fire and brimstone of hell by repeating some facts about Jesus in a ten-second prayer. Salvation in my mind was all about escaping something and nothing more.

The writer Luke recounts a time when Jesus encountered a well-known and extremely wealthy tax collector. The religious elites and fanatics had managed to convince people that this man, because of his status and wealth, was outside the scope of God's love and grace. Luke then goes on to share that this *sinner* was so curious about Jesus that he went to great measures to meet him, and upon doing so, he came to his senses and committed to righting his ways—not in the simple words of a ten-second prayer or the reiteration of a few facts about Jesus, but in the way he began to live. It was by his actions, actions prompted by a change

29

of heart, that Jesus claimed today salvation had "come to this house."[10]

The word *salvation* doesn't just mean the escape *from* something; it's much bigger and more comprehensive than that. It's actually an inclusive word that can also mean deliverance, rescue, safety, preservation, healing, wholeness, and soundness. Yes, it means being rescued *from* but it also means being rescued *into*.[11]

In the movie *Cast Away*, the character played by Tom Hanks uses a raft to escape the island upon which he had been stranded. After this daring escape, he's on the raft in what would have been his final days. It's over, he is worn out, but lying on his back, he slowly raises his hand as a large ship passes near him. It is here that he is rescued—rescued *from* the raging sea, rescued *from* himself. But he is also rescued *into* safety and well-being, *into* a place where he can heal and get whole again, a place where he can then begin to help others. If you recall, once rescued, he begins to see things he never saw before. His life changes; he becomes someone different.

Salvation is not simply a reiteration of the facts of Jesus, or knowing them just so you can get into heaven. The concept of *salvation* is not a Monopoly game where you can play your get-out-of-jail-free card when all is said and done. Thankfully, it's much deeper than that. At its very core, salvation is a way of life; it's a way of being. Salvation is the God-ordained art of being rescued from ourselves, from a Godless now and future. It's also

---

10   Luke 19:1–10.

11   Vine's Expository Dictionary of Biblical Words; The Expositor's Bible Commentary.

the process of being rescued into a new life where we're not the center of the universe, a life of willing service and sacrifice, of extraordinary mission and purpose—a life profoundly sold out to following in the footsteps of Jesus by tangibly addressing the needs of the poor, the hungry, and the homeless of this world as we seek to make things right. This is what Jesus meant when he said, "Today, *salvation* has come into this house."

• **Repent** (the God-ordained art of morphing into)

One day, not that long ago, my brother and I were walking to a University of Michigan football game; it was a long walk (we're too cheap to pay for parking). As we walked along chatting about the game, a Christian street evangelist confronted us. He was carrying a sign that read, "Repent today or else," and his verbal assaults were somewhat threatening. Following us in the street, he went on to explain (scream) that if we refused to repent of our sins, we would burn in a place of hellfire and brimstone. He went on and on; it seemed like it would never end. So, stepping out into the street, I asked him, "If your God is so gracious, why are you so angry?" This really set him off, but my brother and I moved on without further incident. According to some, *repentance* is about fear and guilt, and again, all we need to do is recite a written prayer, and we we're no longer facing eternal damnation; we're in.

Like the word salvation, *repent* (or the idea of repentance) is not simply the reciting of a prayer just so you can know you're going to heaven. Religious fanatics who use fear, guilt, and intimidation to get more converts have hijacked the word; its meaning is much deeper than they espouse.

Repentance (*metanoia*, Greek) means to change; to make a turn-around; to begin walking in the other direction; a "change of mind accompanied by remorse and a change of one's direction in life." In other words, repenting is no casual endeavor; it's monumentally life changing.[12]

The writer Luke recounts the story of a guy by the name of John, who when confronted by the religious elites and fanatics of his day, became agitated and called them a bunch of venomous snakes, hypocrites who claimed repentance without having a true change of heart and subsequent behavior. Unlike the religious leaders, however, the crowds who were also listening to John were moved and began to ask what they needed to do. At these requests, John went on to suggest behaviors that must be *in keeping* with repentance.[13] In other words, repenting is not simply an intellectual assent or mental agreement to a few facts about Jesus; it's so much more.

Repentance is much deeper than most realize. It's not just about forgiveness and destination. It's about wholeness and the trajectory of one's entire life; when we repent, everything begins to change—our hearts, our thinking, our vision, our desires, our hearing, and over time our behavior.

---

12   Vine's Expository Dictionary of Biblical Words, W.E. Vine (Editor), Thomas Nelson Publishers.
13   Luke 3:7–14.

In thinking about this, I am reminded of the British parliamentarian William Wilberforce (1759-1833). Wilberforce was a well-known and well-respected scholar and orator, a man of substantial resources, who while serving as an influential politician became extremely curious about a group known as the evangelicals—Christ followers who embraced a deep concern for the poor, the homeless, and those suffering from the evils of slavery. Wilberforce was deeply moved by their compassion and followership of Jesus, and as a result, he entered their cause and adopted their Christ-following way of life. In essence, he repented, and while it would take him the sum of his life to overturn the British position, policies, and practice of the slave trade, he was successful. His efforts, along with those of many other evangelicals, led to the Slavery Abolition Act of 1833, which abolished slavery in most of the British Empire. Wilberforce died three days after hearing that the passage of the act through Parliament was assured.[14]

So, repentance is a change of heart and mind, an entrance into a life of *process* and continuous *morphing*, as God shapes and reshapes the essence of who we are. Our relationship with God, and the art of repentance, is somewhat like a marriage; there's the marriage *event*, the wedding day, and then more important, there's the marriage *process*, a life of working things out, enjoying successes, and struggling through challenges together. In the process, we grow into something that is greater than the sum of

---

14   Amazing Grace, Eric Metaxas (2007), Harper San Francisco.

our parts. Repentance is this process—it never ends—and along the way, we are changed; we become someone different.

Repentance is what God does in us as we faithfully follow him.

- *Faith* (an open invitation from God to merge trust and dependence)

Faith is a funny word; it is a universal word that is easily applied to almost any circumstance from sports to opera. After all, faith can move mountains, right? Just keep the faith! You got to believe! Hang in there baby and hold on to your faith!

Faith is used as a comfort word and rightfully so.

Faith (*pistis*, Greek) means trust, trustworthiness, a bringing together of belief and the contents, or object, of one's belief.[15]

As it relates to faith, I'm reminded of a time when Peter, one of Jesus's closest and sometimes most challenging followers, asked him a question. Thinking that he was more than law-abiding, Peter asked Jesus if he should forgive someone up to seven times; his question actually offered an answer in that three times was all the religious law required. I suspect Peter was trying to impress Jesus with his willingness to go far beyond what the religious law required. Jesus's answer, however, was more than Peter expected. Jesus explained by illustration that mercy and forgiveness should

---

15   Vine's Expository Dictionary of Biblical Words, W.E. Vine (Editor), Thomas Nelson Publishers.

be offered to others to the same extent that it is offered to us by God—that is, unlimited and without prejudice.[16]

At first glance, one would think that the conversation between Peter and Jesus was simply about mercy and forgiveness. Indeed, their conversation was about those things, but not surprisingly, Jesus takes Peter deeper. In the last phrase of their conversation, Jesus went on to explain that *mercy and forgiveness come from the heart*, from a place deeper inside the human soul.

I'm convinced that mercy and forgiveness are like bananas and apples; they are manifestations of something deeper, products of something bigger; this is why you find fruit in the produce section of the market. It's the same with mercy and forgiveness; they too are manifestations of something deeper—products of healthy roots. So, as it turns out, Jesus's conversation with Peter was actually about *faith*, and from their conversation, we can see that *faith* is something found deep inside. Jesus was showing Peter that *faith* is much bigger than the law; it is far reaching and much more liberating. *Faith* is something we experience at our very core and willingly enter into. *Faith* is a humble, ongoing walk or conversation with God that leads to a life of unexplainable trust and total dependence upon him. It is faith that produces trust, and trust is the root from which mercy and forgiveness emerge, not the law or our ability to follow it.

The religious elites trust and depend on their ability to follow the letter of the law, all of the rules, and therefore, they expect

---

16   Matthew 18:21–35.

everyone else to do the same. They outright demand that others do the same and if they don't they ridicule and persecute them. In both cases, the object of their faith is the law and their ability to follow it. Sincere doubt, continual questioning, and honest inquiry are signs of weakness or, as they would proclaim, a lack of faith. In reality, nothing could be further from the truth.

What about faith and the religiously indifferent? Having walked away from the dreams and desires of their Father, much like the younger son in our earlier story, the religiously indifferent trust in themselves, in their own ability to make sense of life and circumstances; in their own ability to cope with the trials, tragedies, and successes of life. The object of their faith can be a moving target or, at best, a faith in faith itself. For them, hope can easily become an elusive dream, a never-ending journey across bridges to nowhere in particular.

In the Hebrew scriptures, also known as the Old Testament in Christian circles, there is a story of three young men who found themselves serving a king in a foreign land; they were being held captive by no fault of their own. One day, the king, who was extremely demanding, had a larger-than-life statue of himself built so that his entire kingdom could worship him. He then took it one step further and instructed his guard to punish those who refused to worship this statue, and the punishment was death by furnace.

These three young men, however, were devout followers of the God who created the heavens and the earth, the God who is at the center of the Jewish faith. To them, there was only one true God worthy of worship, and it was not the king. So, when they refused to worship the king's statue, the guards brought them before the king and explained the situation. The king, who appreciated what these three young men did for him, offered them a second chance, but again, they refused to worship the statue. The king then became furious and proudly asked them if there was any god who could rescue them from his wrath. It is here, in the reply of these three young men, that we get the purest definition of faith:

"Our God, the God we serve, can rescue us from your hands," they said, but they went on to explain that even if God didn't rescue them from the furnace, they would not bow down and worship the king or his statue.[17] Their faith was not a faith in the law, not a faith in faith, nor was it a faith in themselves. Their faith was a convergence of their belief and the object of that belief: the one true God of all creation.

Not knowing that God would ultimately deliver them from the furnace unharmed, their faith was a merging of unwavering trust and total dependence on Him.

Faith is not the absence of doubt, nor is it an elusive endeavor that leads nowhere in particular. More important than faith itself is the object of one's faith; it is here that the religion of Jesus is unique. Genuine faith is an invitation by Jesus to merge trust and dependence on him willingly. It is here that faith transcends circumstance and situation; it is here that Jesus says, "Come to me all who are weary and worn out by the impossible task of obeying

17   Daniel 3:18.

the law, all the rules"; it is here that Jesus simply says, "Come and rest, rest in your faith in me."

In his now well-known 1959 speech, Vince Lombardi, the legendary coach of the Green Bay Packers, began the preseason with these opening words, "*Gentleman, this is a football.*" As many have already commented, the point he was trying to make was the necessity of getting back to the fundamentals, the basics.

We now began our exploration of the religion of Jesus.

PART TWO | *Religion and Life as It Was Meant to Be*

———————

[Jesus said] The thief comes only in order to steal, kill, and destroy. I have come in order that you might have life—life in all its fullness.

—John, one of the Apostles of Jesus (John 10:10)

INTRODUCTION | *a cosmic love story...*

There seem to be several misconceptions about the Bible and why it was written. Some see it as a book of rules, while others view it as nothing more than ancient literature. There are those who see the Bible as the handbook for daily living, and others who look at it as a guide to life, both the eternal and the present, earthly life. The range of interpretations and uses are as vast as the time it took to write it. While its veracity and trustworthiness is for another book—of which there are many—the challenges of history, culture, language, scientific discovery, and the time distance between those who wrote it and those who now read it are paramount to understanding its message.

What gets lost in the seemingly never-ending technical biblical arguments, however, is the overriding purpose and intent of its writing, the larger story behind it all. When you step back and take a panoramic view of it, what you see is a never-ending, cosmic love story. At its very foundation, you discover a God who joyfully creates and a people who willfully walk away, and then you read about the very same creator God graciously and relentlessly pursuing those who walked away, those he deeply loves: us. It's what I call a *red thread* theme that runs through all sixty-six books.

Maybe reading the Bible is much like viewing the Grand Canyon. You could spend your entire life rambling through and nitpicking every rock, every nook and cranny, every valley, every geological anomaly, every first-glance scientific contradiction, and totally miss the grand nature and mystical beauty of it all. Could it be that the cosmic love story that runs through the entire Bible is like the Colorado River that runs through the Grand Canyon? The river is what gives the canyon life, much like the red thread of God's love story does to the Bible.

In our ongoing religious debates, bantering, and discourse, maybe we've all missed the bigger picture: that the life Jesus offers to those who desire to walk humbly in his footsteps is a life of unparalleled freedom. In part two of the religion of Jesus, you will see the heart of the one true God, the creator God who loves us all beyond measure. Jesus himself said, "I have come in order that you might have life—life in all its fullness." Unlike the religion of the religious others, the religion that Jesus offers is an invitation that welcomes *everyone* into the mix. For at its very core, it is a religion that revolves around the holistic needs of anyone and everyone.

With open hearts and minds, the religious elite, fanatics, and indifferent can all catch a glimpse of God's desire for *all of us* to live in the midst of his cosmic and compassionate love story. New chapters are being written every day.

As you read and digest the rest of this book, may the next chapter written be yours.

THE RELIGION OF JESUS | *back to the future...*

A Jesus I Can Live With...

If you read long enough and search hard enough, you can find someone who agrees with you, someone who validates your ideas and personal beliefs, whatever they may be. It's no different when it comes to beliefs about the person of Jesus. His identity is at question every Christmas and Easter.

It seems as if there are many well-intended people, good people, who consider themselves very Christian and very religious, who have constructed for themselves an identity of Jesus that is palatable, safe, easier to swallow, and free from the more challenging and difficult teachings that he offered. My fear is that they have crafted a caricature of Jesus they can live with as opposed to falling in love with the Jesus they can't truly live without.

The religion of Jesus is intellectually demanding and emotionally overwhelming. However, if we muster up the courage and take the time to closely examine the fullness of his identity and character, we begin to understand that belief in him is a paradigm shift of cosmic proportions, one that pushes us off the paved road of unchallenged thought and lifestyle.

The religion of Jesus is an invitation into a way of life, a kingdom-on-earth experience whereby we simply follow the king in all his fullness and in all the demands of his unwavering love. Ironically, it is here that we discover a life of unparalleled freedom.

Every worthwhile journey has to start somewhere, so to capture the nature and essence of his religion, we must begin with his identity: a cornerstone of the Christian faith. By the way, we are not the first to wonder about his identity. Let's go back to the future.

The Religion of Jesus Was/Is Founded in His Unavoidable Identity…

In the early goings of the movement started by Jesus and immediately after his death and resurrection, there was an extremely large gathering of Jews who began to express a deep interest in him. So, one writer took some time to explain where Jesus came from: the writer of a New Testament book called Hebrews. In the introduction to this lengthy book, the writer describes the identity of Jesus by looking at his existence long before everything we see could be seen. In fact, he quite clearly explains that it is Jesus who created it all.[18]

You can dig deeper into this crazy idea in John 1:1–14. After reading about the creative power of Jesus (verses 1–4), it's fun to compare the entrance of John the Baptist who *came*

---

18   Hebrews 1:1–3.

into the world (verse 6) and that of Jesus who *became* flesh (verse 14). These two words are critical in understanding the two very different entrances into this world of Jesus and John the Baptist. Briefly, the word *came* and the word *became* are huge in defining and understanding how John and Jesus arrived on the scene. *Became,* the process by which Jesus arrived, means that he morphed into something from something, that he preexisted his human form. The word *came* (into this world), however, indicates that John's existence started when he was born.

From these two early writers and firsthand followers of Jesus we learn:

- *Through* Jesus, God fashioned the universe. Jesus was the agent of the creative act; he was there at the beginning of all creation and therefore preexisted it. He has a vested interest in what went wrong with it and how to restore it.
- Jesus is the radiance and exact representation of God; he is not simply an addition to a long line of religious prophets and teachers; unlike them, he is God.[19]
- Jesus sustains all life and existence; he always has and always will. He didn't simply come and go. He is not an uninterested party. He was back then and he still is today on an incredible mission of rescue, restoration, and relief (more on this later).

---

19   For an in-depth look into the identity options of Jesus, I highly recommend you read the classic work of C. S. Lewis, Mere Christianity.

To be sure, the religion of Jesus revolves around his identity. He thought us up before time began and created us. But why begin here? If Jesus is the creator God of the universe, he can be trusted. We can trust his love; we can trust his promise; we can trust his plans; we can trust his motives when he asks us to do something; moreover, we can trust the religion he invites us into.

This is why we (must) begin with the identity of Jesus.

The Religion of Jesus Was/Is Centered on His Heart of Unwavering Compassion...

Have you ever watched *Undercover Boss*? It's a show about CEOs who disguise themselves and then take on an entry-level job so they can experience what's really going on in their businesses. The few that I have watched are pretty cool and quite moving. But this is not really an original idea, is it?

Jesus, the one who created the heavens and the earth, was willing to drop everything, enter the world he created, and touch a single life—not because he had to, but because he was filled with compassion. Have you ever really wondered *why* Jesus needed to enter the scene? For a peek into the answer, simply examine two episodes in the early ministry of Jesus (you can read them on your own; they require very little explanation).

- **Mark 1:40–42**: It's a moving story of a time when Jesus encountered a man with leprosy. As such, the man was considered unclean and unworthy of God's love by the religious elites and fanatics. Moved with compassion, however, Jesus reached out and touched the man; it was most likely the first time this man had been physically touched by the hand of another. Imagine what he must have felt inside when Jesus made him *clean*. He was healed both physically and emotionally.

- **Luke 15:20**: Here, Jesus explains that how the rejected father had compassion on the son who demanded his inheritance only to squander it away, remember? In the verses that follow, Jesus points to the reaction of the elder son, who was outright angry at the father for hosting a party for the younger son who returned home. It is the elder son who typifies the religion of the religious others. Unlike them, Jesus embraces others with compassion.

These two stories highlight the vast difference between the religion of the religious elite, the religion of the religious fanatics, the religion of the religiously indifferent, and the religion of Jesus. But again, why did Jesus enter the scene? Did he come to abolish religion by being nonreligious or even irreligious? As fashionable as it may be today, this is not why he *became*.

Jesus *became* for many reasons, all of which are seated in his deep love and unwavering compassion for the entire human race. He knew that religion and the life that came with it had morphed into something ugly. The religion that God loves so dearly had become a religion that couldn't care less about those buried by the slow death of poverty and rejection. The religion of the religious others had established an "I'm in and you're out" system; they created for themselves an egocentric, safe path whereby they could ignore the pleas and cries of those who suffer, those who by no fault of their own live on scraps, those who are broken and hurting. On the other hand, the religion of Jesus is a relief effort that centers upon the physical and emotional needs of those on the religious fringe: the rejected and forgotten, the poor and homeless, the hungry and orphaned, and those who have been forgotten, shamed, and ridiculed by the religious others.

Unlike the others, Jesus leads with heartfelt and heartwarming compassion.

This is why Christ followers try to walk in his footsteps and lead with the same compassion. They too have been touched by his compassionate hand—the tender hand of mercy and grace; the tender hand of wholeness, healing, and care; the tender hand of new life and freedom from the religion of the religious others. They follow his lead, not because they have to, but because they *get to*, and this is the vast difference between the religion of Jesus and the others we have discussed. Following and obeying the words of Jesus is not an obligation, nor is it a duty; it is an off-the-charts privilege and an entrance into a life of unparalleled freedom.

Maybe you're reading this and need to experience that loving touch of Jesus; if so, keep reading, because once touched, you're invited into the mix; it's a risky endeavor to say the least, one that is designed to rescue, restore, and relieve.

Once touched, forever changed. This is the religion of Jesus.

The Religion of Jesus Was / Is Intentionally Apolitical...

Not that long ago, I was having coffee with a great friend and trial running partner who had grown tired of religion and what was being espoused on Sunday mornings at church. As we sat talking about our next endurance race, he asked whether Jesus, if he were here today, would be a conservative Republican or a liberal Democrat. We talk about this kind of stuff regularly; he makes me think, not just outside the box, but also beyond the box. He has helped me more than he knows.

It took approximately three hundred years for the wheels to fall off the wagon, but once Christianity was "legitimized" by Constantine in AD 313, it began a slow roll downhill. By the middle five hundreds, the religious and political leaders had locked arms in mission and purpose. Christianity had been hijacked by politics, and it would take centuries to recover; some would say it hasn't.

Let there be no doubt, religion and politics make strange bedfellows.

One day, when asked about paying taxes to Caesar, Jesus looked at a coin with Caesar's portrait and inscription on it. Refusing to get caught up in politics, he simply said, "Give to Caesar what is Caesar's and give to God what is God's. It's that simple."[20]

---

20   Luke 20:19–26.

It seems as if the Christian religion goes wild every five hundred years or so; it's no different with Christianity today. Religious leaders use politics and politicians use religion to get their way, to advance their cause, and to gain more control. However, when you study the sum of his life and the essence of his priorities, you'll discover that Jesus was not a conservative Republican, a liberal Democrat, a moderate Independent, Libertarian, Wall Street protestor, or Tea Party member. He was not a Socialist, Communist, president, CEO, Fascist, Capitalist, free-marketer, dictator, or monarch. Furthermore, when the religion he founded and the politics that surround it occupy the same bed, the religion of Jesus gets subverted and stolen. It loses its focus and intended purpose; it becomes a tool for more power and control, just another way to get more votes and/or foster an agenda in keeping with one's ideology or way of life.

This is dangerous.

The religion of Jesus does not belong to a political party, nor is it an American phenomenon. It is a global movement that began long before the birth of the American dream. The religion of Jesus is found anywhere and everywhere. It is not dependent upon any government or the politicians that come with it; Jesus transcends culture, language, nationality, philosophy, socioeconomics, ethnicity, gender, and geography.

The religion of Jesus transcends government, politics, and personal agenda.

The Religion of Jesus Was/Is Far from a Casual Endeavor...

The teachings of Jesus are not easy; they can be demanding and seemingly over the top. It is common today, just as it was in his time, for people to walk away and move on because of Jesus's call for living a life different than most.[21] With regularity, Jesus taught his followers to view life and conduct through the lens of morality, ethics, purity, generosity, mercy, unconditional forgiveness, love of one's enemy, sacrifice, humility, kindness, obedience, and faithfulness. He invites everyone into a life of faith that is a merging together of unwavering trust and sometimes not so easy dependence.

But here's the rub. The religion of the religious others promotes the belief that through obeying Jesus, you garner his acceptance; when you obey the rules, you're in, and if you don't, you're out. By now, you should be well aware that this runs in direct opposition with the religion of Jesus.

To illustrate this further, next to the cross of Jesus upon which he was executed, there were two others, criminals who were being executed for their crimes. One of them, hoping to gain favor from the crowd, joined them in hurling insults at Jesus. The other criminal, however, after recognizing the innocence of Jesus and his own guilt, simply looked at Jesus and asked to be remembered when Jesus entered the kingdom. To this, Jesus responded, "Today you will be with me in paradise."[22] I often

---

21   In John 6:60–67; many walked away from him because his teachings were difficult.
22   Luke 23:39–43.

wonder how many times this man went to church, paid his tithes, read his Bible, said the four-part prayer, received Communion, got baptized, went on mission trips, served in a church, played the game, or said the right words.

Was he even religious?

This man wasn't accepted by Jesus because he obeyed the religious rules out of duty and obligation; he was unconditionally embraced by Jesus simply because he lovingly reached out to him. The religious others use fear and control. Jesus, on the other hand, extends his compassionate hand of sacrificial love; the difference is that simple.

The religion of Jesus is an invitation into a life of grace and freedom, and that is why his followers embrace his teachings—not because they must and not because they are seeking his acceptance. They obey because they can, they get to, they want to, they love to, and they know that when they fail, Jesus picks them up again and again; when they fail, they *fail forward* into an abundance of grace, in limitless and reckless love, and in unwarranted but ever-so-welcomed mercy. And in the midst of this unparalleled freedom, every part of our life becomes fair game.

This is the religion of Jesus: an entry into life-altering freedom.

The Religion of Jesus at Its Best Is a Divine Dance...

Flashback—my brother and I are in the basement of XYZ Bible Church lying about our "sinful" life as teens. Remember, this was when I learned to play the game—being religious on Sunday and something very different most other days. It was extremely frustrating, but it was also an experience that would prompt a seminary paper "Sinners in the Hands of an Angry Preacher." My paper was a play on words, taken from a famous sermon entitled, "Sinners in the Hands of an Angry God." The professor didn't think it was funny.

When did the word *sinner* become such a derogatory and inflammatory word? When did it morph into a pejorative term of judgment and condemnation? It's not an accident that in the book of Luke, the word *sinner* is often found in quotes; his intent was to highlight how the religion of the religious elite and the religion of the religious fanatics had managed to build walls instead of bridges—walls of hatred, walls of separation and disdain. I wonder if they picketed funerals with "God hates (fill in the blank)" signs?

The religion of Jesus stands in stark contrast to that of all the others we have discussed. His was simple and yet substantive. He never wavered in his mission and purpose. He never allowed the religion of the others to derail him from his deep-seated love of the world (John 3:16) and his broken heart for the one (John 8:2–11).

Remember the writer Luke recalling a moving story told by Jesus of a compassionate father running out joyfully to embrace his wayward son, his younger son who demanded all that his father had worked for only to squander it away? Remember the father's unwavering compassion, the warm, judgeless embrace and the celebration that followed? This is typical of the religion of Jesus and yet unexplainably nauseates those who subscribe to the religion of the others (i.e., the response of elder son).[23]

Have you ever watched a young girl dance with her daddy? With her standing on the top of his feet, they move with the music; slowly, her steps become his as they learn to move as one, and when you look at their faces, pure joy is etched on both. Is it possible that this is what Jesus had in mind: a divine dance, a tender moment when a *sinner* who has simply drifted away meets a Father who deeply loves her or him? It is for me; like many of you, I was once this wayward son, but now I'm captivated by the Jesus I never knew growing up. As my dance with him unfolds, my steps are slowly being transformed into his; there is nothing else like it.

This is the religion of Jesus, the Jesus we can't truly live without.

The Religion of Jesus Is an Open-Ended, Nonjudgmental Invitation to Anyone and Everyone in the Room...

So, sitting at my desk working through a few e-mails, I see one from a good friend who is reading through a few of my early notes as it relates to this book. The e-mail reads, *"Ron, do you have any compassion for the religious elites or the religious fanatics?"* It was a question that at first puzzled me, but the longer it sat there,

---

23   See The Prodigal God, Timothy Keller (2008). Penguin Group Publishing.

the deeper it sank in; it was not a good feeling, and the all-too-familiar knot in my stomach began to tighten.

In March of 2002, I was invited to join a team of short-term missionaries on a trip to South Africa, and as it would turn out, this trip would deconstruct my view of what Jesus calls the Good News. The flight was an exhausting nineteen hours, and once we finally arrived at our destination, we sat in on a cultural and ministry orientation class. During the class, our missionary hosts began to explain the culture of the people we were going to be working with for the next few weeks; it was fascinating as we learned about the vastly different cultural beliefs and religious practices of a group of people who lived on the other side of the planet. Our host went on to explain that as we traveled through the villages and helped people with their daily chores, it was okay to ask questions about family history, culture, and beliefs about religion. It was going to be a great trip.

As the orientation unfolded, however, we were told that it was our role to present the Good News of Jesus and then explain how their religious and cultural practice of communicating with their dead ancestors was in violation of the teachings of the Bible; it was not proper Christian behavior and as such, must be stopped. The knot in my stomach began to surface, but I was a guest and needed to keep my opinions to myself.

For the few first days of our travels and interaction with the people who lived in a village nearby, I behaved and stayed in line with the desires of the missionary leaders. Each evening, as we sat in our small groups to discuss the events of the day, my frustration grew. To me, the Good News we were sharing was far from good news to those who had simply been practicing many generations of cultural belief. To them, the Good News was not good news; it was culturally offensive.

So a week into our trip, I decided to go off on my own and help a man by the name of Petros; he lived in a three-room wooden shack with a tarpaper roof on a small tract of land. As I walked by, he was preparing his garden. After asking for permission, I joined him in shoveling and raking for most of the day; we laughed and laughed as he tried to teach me various words in his language. We had a great time. Upon returning the next morning, I found him brewing tea. He invited me to join him. With the help of an interpreter, we sat and chatted for hours. He shared his life; I shared mine. It was rich.

As it turned out, Petros was a churchgoing man, and when the topic of communicating with our ancestors came up, it finally dawned on me; we all have cultural beliefs we bring to the religious table. So I went on to explain how we in the United States have TVs, phones, and computers in almost every room; how most families have at least two or three cars; how our homes are fifteen to twenty times the size of his with fewer people living in them; how we throw away more food than we eat; how our homes typically have two or three bathrooms, a two-car garage, hot and cold running water, and weekly trash pickup; how we spend more on our pets than they spend on their families; how our personal debt is a thousand times more than he makes a year; how we have more comfort features than money can buy; and then how when we want more, we sell our house, go deeper in debt, and buy a bigger one. Needless to say, he was shocked and overwhelmed!

Both Petros and I learned something that day; when we enter into a relationship with Jesus, we bring the sum total of who we are with us; we bring to him all of our history and experience, all of our religious beliefs, all of our behaviors, all of our cultural mores and biases, all of our dreams, all of our fears, and all of our preconceived notions of how life should unfold; we can't help it.

His cultural practice was ancestor worship; my cultural practice was materialism. We were not that different. The Good News for both of us is that Jesus has better ideas as to how we should live and over time, he will help both of us understand. The Good News must be good news to everyone, or it's not good news at all.

It seems as if knots in my stomach mean there must be something to learn.

As it turns out, the answer to my friend's question is a resounding yes; I do have compassion for those who hold to the religion of the religious others. My hope beyond hope is that they will enter the dance, that they will join those of us who have surrendered the sum of who we are, our pre-Jesus religion, to the one who transforms, the one who slowly shaves off our rough edges of judgmentalism, criticism, narrow-mindedness, jealousy, short-sightedness, hatred, and fear of the unknown—to the king and founder of Christianity. It is here that the young-earth theologian and old-earth theologian can freely discuss their various views, chuckle at the differences, and join hands as they mutually embrace a religion that revolves around the holistic needs of others. When it works well, it's a sight to behold.

As I mentioned earlier, I'm not sure when it happened, but long before becoming a Christ follower, I somehow knew that you could tell what a person truly believed by his or her actions over the course of time; religion is an unavoidable binding together of belief and practice. Therefore, whether we care to admit it or not, everyone is religious. But it's not the religion of Jesus that gets us in trouble; it's the religion that we all bring to it. This is where it can sometimes spin out of control; we create for ourselves a religion of the religious others, and before you know it, the damage is done.

This is why the religion of Jesus is an open-ended, nonjudgmental invitation to anyone and everyone in the room.

FINAL THOUGHTS | *a hat moment in kenya. . .*

For the Son of Man came to find [rescue] and restore the lost.

—Jesus, the Son of God
(as told by Luke, in Luke 19:10)

In March of 2006, two great friends and I journeyed to
Kenya to help with the establishment of a mission station (a deep
water well and a building to be used as a school and church).
While there, we visited a potential mission station site and joined
in on the dedication of the land. As is customary, the visitors, like
my friends and I, sat up front in chairs, in the shade. Everyone
else, Kenyans who would actually use the mission station, sat on
the ground in the hot sun. Then, while everyone else sat there
in the scorching heat, each visitor was invited to step up to the
podium and say a few words of encouragement.

The person who sat in the seat next to me was an American
missionary to Africa, ready to travel back home; he was a nice
guy. I was scheduled to say a few words after him. He stepped up
to the podium and demanded that all those who were sitting on
the ground in the hot sun remove their hats. Apparently, the Bible
says that it is disrespectful to wear a hat in the house of God.

He waited until everyone sitting there was hatless, baking and sweating in the 105-degree heat before he commenced speaking of obeying God's rules and the need to recite the four-part prayer. He went on and on.

As I was sitting there, my heart and soul harkened back to XYZ Bible Church, to the angry street fanatic who demanded repentance, to the religious others who miss the point of it all. Visibly upset and heartbroken, I found it was my turn to say a few words, so I walked up to the podium with hat in hand. For what seemed like an eternity, I stood there in silence looking into the eyes of the sweaty, haggard faces of people who just loved Jesus, real people who longed for freedom and release, people who had bigger challenges than wearing a worthless hat in God's house.

So putting my hat back on my head, I invited them to do the same, explaining that Jesus, in all of his love and compassion, offers of a life of unparalleled freedom, freedom from the rules and regulations dictated by the religious others, and then sat back down. I'm told that it took three to four minutes. You should have seen the ear-to-ear smiles on their faces, the profound relief in their collective eyes, and the tears of joy running down our cheeks. I was a mess.

In the depth of the human soul is a desperate longing for the touch that only Jesus can offer; there is a void inside that only the religion of Jesus can fill. It is found in his extraordinarily profound and yet wildly simple mission:

- To *rescue* those of us lost in a sea of brokenness, shame, loneliness, wealth, poverty, failure, success, insignificance, frustration, religious bondage, fear, doubt, and frustration—religious or irreligious;
- To begin *restoring* those of us who have been rescued— restoring our identity, purpose, life's meaning, and freedom back to our original God-ordained image;
- To *relieve* the sufferings of the poor, the homeless, the orphaned, and the hungry by tangibly addressing their real needs, and moreover, making things right.

It was the Kenyan hat moment that solidified my commitment to escaping the religions of the religious others and thereby entering into the ever-challenging world of the religion that Jesus offers to us all.

My life was changed. I'm becoming someone different. This is the religion of Jesus.

NEXT STEPS | *what are you waiting for?*

One of my greatest thrills is teaching, helping people dig deeper into the person and life of Christ so as to learn who he was, what he did, and why it is so life-critical to fall in love with him and live as he lived on this blue marble. Teaching for the sake of information acquisition, however, is simply a cosmic waste of time and energy.

So, with this in mind, if you feel so inclined, you have a couple of options:

a) You can go to www.RonGelaude.com and investigate further;

b) You can work through the following using a journal, a notebook, or the margins of this book:

1. In one sentence, what if anything did you learn in each section?

2. How did this *insight* affect your thinking?

3. What will this *insight* prompt you to change in your own life?

4. How are you going to *go about it* or enter into this particular life change?

5. What other resources do you need to garner in order to move forward?

So what's holding you back from a divine dance with Jesus? Is it fear, doubt, not yet having the full picture, or the possible ridicule from your friends or family? Or maybe it's the damage that has been done by the various groups we've discussed.

Whatever the hesitation, you need to know that you're not alone; many of us are just like you. This is why it's called faith. It does not require a giant leap of faith, but a one-small-step-at-a-time faith, a trusting faith in the like-no-other Jesus. In him, you'll never be disappointed.

So, go ahead, simply look up into the heavens and tell him that you love him for who he is and what he has done; ask him to guide you in life as you seek to love him and walk in his footsteps. To help you in this journey, I highly recommend that you begin reading the entire book of John using a translation called The Message. Take your time and enjoy every minute, and if at all possible, please find someone to take this journey with you— preferably in a local church where compassion rules! It won't take you long to figure it out.

Finally, with the religion of Jesus, the life change never ends. We're all in the process of becoming. To this line of thinking my older brother comments, "My life change took place suddenly, over a period of twenty years." How cool is this?

AFTERWORD

Thanks for reading these scribbles. How far they go is not up to me, but my hope of hopes is that you now have something to think about, something that will prompt you to consider or reconsider the religion that only Jesus offers, the way of life that binds our belief in him with how we live on this earth. Truth is, you can't really separate them, can you?

Everyone is religious, so we all must choose wisely. It's your call.

Finally, this work is dedicated to my lovely and precious wife, who passed during its writing. She lived an incredible life of faith in Jesus despite thirty-six years of constant struggle with systemic lupus, which ultimately stole her life far too soon. She is my inspiration to continue walking in the footsteps of Jesus and the unparalleled freedom he offers; her divine dance with Jesus, the king of kings, is now at its zenith.

—Ron Gelaude, Christ follower

ACKNOWLEDGMENTS
THOSE WHO MAKE IT ALL POSSIBLE

Engaging in any meaningful endeavor requires a network of people who make it all possible. C. S. Lewis defined friends as those who know the dreams of your heart and then regularly speak those dreams back to you. To this truth, I would simply add that friends also help turn your dreams into reality.

My dream-makers are:

- Ken—your never-ending atypical theological questions pushed me off the fence, but this is what brothers are for...
- Don and Martha—thanks for adopting me into your very special family...
- Bob, Meghan, Matt, Brian, Don, Sandy, Drew, and Amy—thanks for your endless encouragement...
- Val and Pam—thanks for keeping me focused and on track...
- Joe and Miranda—thanks for inspiring me...
- Brian—thanks for the off-the-charts research...
- The Connexions crazy sheep—thanks for allowing me to pursue my larger-than-life dreams...
- Thank you Bonnie; we'll dance again in the next life. I promise...

Hey, Mom, I did it...

About the Author and What's on the Horizon

Ron Gelaude is the church-planting pastor (a.k.a., the lead follower) of Connexions Covenant Church in Dexter, Michigan. Connexions Church is affiliated with the Great Lakes Conference of the Evangelical Covenant Church. Ron is a graduate of William Tyndale College (BRE, pastoral studies, 1994); Michigan Theological Seminary (master of theological studies, 1997), and Eastern Michigan University (master of communication studies, 2001). Ron was married to Bonnie Gelaude for thirty-seven years and continues to lead Connexions Church with compassion.

For him *compassion rules!*

What's on the horizon?

- **Crazy Sheep** | *In Pursuit of a Life Worth Living...*
- **The Stone Carver** | *The Reshaping of Who We Are...*
- **When God Says No** | *Or So It Seems...*
- **Second Fiddle** | *Recapturing the Lost Art of Following...*

Ron can be reached at:

- rgelaude@connexionscc.com
- facebook.com/connexionschurch
- compassionrules.com
- rongelaude.com

APPENDIX I
BRIEF OVERVIEW OF RELIGIOUS PERSECUTION BY CHRISTIANS

The *Great Crusades*[24]*

When: 1095–1291

Who Did What: Religiously sanctioned military campaigns were conducted by Roman Catholics against Muslims to retake Jerusalem and the Holy Land.

Sources: "History of the Crusades," an online course from Boise State University by E. L. Skip Knox (http://boisestate. edu/courses/crusades/) and Wikipedia, "Crusades" (http:// en.wikipedia.org/wiki/crusades).

The Inquisition (actually a series of four inquisitions: Medieval, Spanish, Portuguese, and Roman)

When: 1184–1860

Who Did What: Catholic Church bodies used brutal methods of torture and punishment to investigate and punish accusations of heresy and witchcraft (e.g., Joan of Arc was burned at the stake in 1431). Christians persecuted Jews, Muslims, and other Christians. In Spain, a 1492 edict required that Jews must convert to Catholicism, leave the country, or be executed. A similar edict forced Muslims to leave Spain (1609–1614). In the American

---

24   *Research for this section was done by Mr. Brian Clapham, a dear friend.

colonies, local church leaders used these techniques against women and men in the Salem witchcraft trials of 1692.

Sources: New World Encyclopedia, "Inquisition" (http:// www.newworldencyclopedia.org/entry/Inquisition); "Famous American Trials: The Salem Witchcraft Trials of 1692," Douglas O. Linder (http://law2.umkc/edu/faculty/projects/ftrials/ salem/salem.htm).

Forced Conversion of Indigenous Populations
When: 1492–1898
Who Did What: European explorers, beginning with Columbus, sought wealth and spread Christianity through forced "conversions" of native peoples living in the territories they "discovered." In the American Colonies and later the United States, there were many military campaigns against Native Americans justified by religion and the quest for land.
Sources: *A People's History of the United States: 1492–Present*, by Howard Zinn, 2001 (Harper Collins, 1999); "First Nation History," by Daniel N. Paul (http://www.danielnpaul.com/ ChristopherColumbus.html); "The Hole in Our Gospel," by Richard Stearns (Thomas Nelson, 2009), 191.

Religious Persecution in Europe
When: 1550s–1770s
Who Did What: Catholics and Protestants were tortured, murdered, and driven from their communities by each other,

depending on which group had power in that area. Several religious wars occurred between 1560 and 1715. Many who were not killed settled in the American colonies where they could openly and freely practice their religion.

Sources: The History Guide, "Lecture 6: Europe in the Age of Religious Wars, 1560–1715"; *Religion and the Founding of the American Republic*, Library of Congress Publication (1992) (http://www.loc.gov/exhibits/religion/).

Slavery in the Americas
When: 1619–1865

Who Did What: European nations bought and sold African men, women, and children as property and forced them to work on their plantations in the New World under very inhumane conditions. Slavery was justified by many Christians as being the "natural order" of the world. The British Empire abolished slavery in 1833. The United States officially ended slavery in 1865.

Sources: *Amazing Grace: William Wilberforce and the Heroic Campaign to End Slavery*, by Eric Metaxas (Harper San Francisco, 2007). Slavery in America (http://www.slaveryinamerica.org/history/overview.htm).

The German Church's Support of Hitler
When: 1933–1945

Who Did What: Hitler organized a "German Christian" movement within the Protestant Church to support the Nazi goals of removing Jews from Germany as a means to "purify" the Aryan race. This led to the Final Solution, the Holocaust that killed six million Jews. This "cleansing" of the race also meant that other groups of people, such as homosexuals, Gypsies, and people with disabilities, were justifiably murdered because they were a drain on society and the war effort.

Sources: *Bonhoeffer: Pastor, Martyr, Prophet, Spy*, by Eric Metaxas (Thomas Nelson, 2010); United States Holocaust Memorial Museum (http://www.ushmm.org/wlc/en/article.php?Module).

Appendix II
Suggested Reading

Listed below are a few of the authors and books that have profoundly influenced my thinking and life over the past ten years.

Divine Conspiracy, by Dallas Willard

Mere Christianity, by C. S. Lewis

Surprised by Hope, by N. T. Wright

The Prodigal God, by Timothy Keller

The Hole in the Gospel, by Richard Stearns

The Barbarian Way, by Erwin McManus

Missional Church, by Darrell L. Gruder

Too Small to Ignore, by Dr. Wess Stafford

The Presence of the Future, by George Ladd

And last but not even close to being the least:

The New Scofield Study Bible (NIV)
Back jacket...

There are dozens of books out there that proudly claim, without reservation, that Jesus was irreligious or even sacrilegious. I suppose it's in vogue to make such observations, but, in reality, nothing could be further from the truth. Jesus's life and teachings show he was a far cry from being irreligious or sacrilegious.

Yes, he was profoundly frustrated and angry with the religious leaders of the day and what religion had become, but his mission was not one of dismissing religion.

His mission was one of boldly reclaiming religion and all the beauty that comes with it. It is here that hope surfaces; there is a religion worth considering, a religion worth *living*.

It's called the religion of Jesus.

—Ron Gelaude

Made in the USA
San Bernardino, CA
29 April 2015